ED EMBERLEY'S
Drawing Book of
HALLOWEEN

LITTLE, BROWN AND COMPANY

New York ❧ Boston

Copyright © 1980 by Edward R. Emberley

Cover and title page illustrations copyright © 2006 by Edward R. Emberley

Little, Brown and Company

Time Warner Book Group

1271 Avenue of the Americas, New York, NY, 10020

Visit our Web site at www.lb-kids.com

First Revised Paperback Edition: August 2006

10   9   8   7   6   5   4   3   2   1

LCCN 95-777929

ISBN: 0-316-78977-1

WKT

Printed in China

Previously published as *Ed Emberley's Halloween Drawing Book*

2

IF YOU CAN DRAW THESE SIMPLE SHAPES

$(\triangle \ O \ \square \ D \cdot I \ L \ \wedge \ C)$

HERE'S A GOOD CHANCE THAT YOU WILL BE ABLE TO DRAW AT LEAST MOST OF THE THINGS IN THIS BOOK .

STEP-BY-STEP INSTRUCTIONS SHOW YOU HOW.

A HAPPY ORANGE

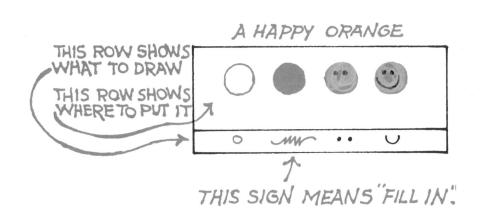

THIS ROW SHOWS WHAT TO DRAW

THIS ROW SHOWS WHERE TO PUT IT

THIS SIGN MEANS "FILL IN".

A HAPPY ORANGE, WALKING

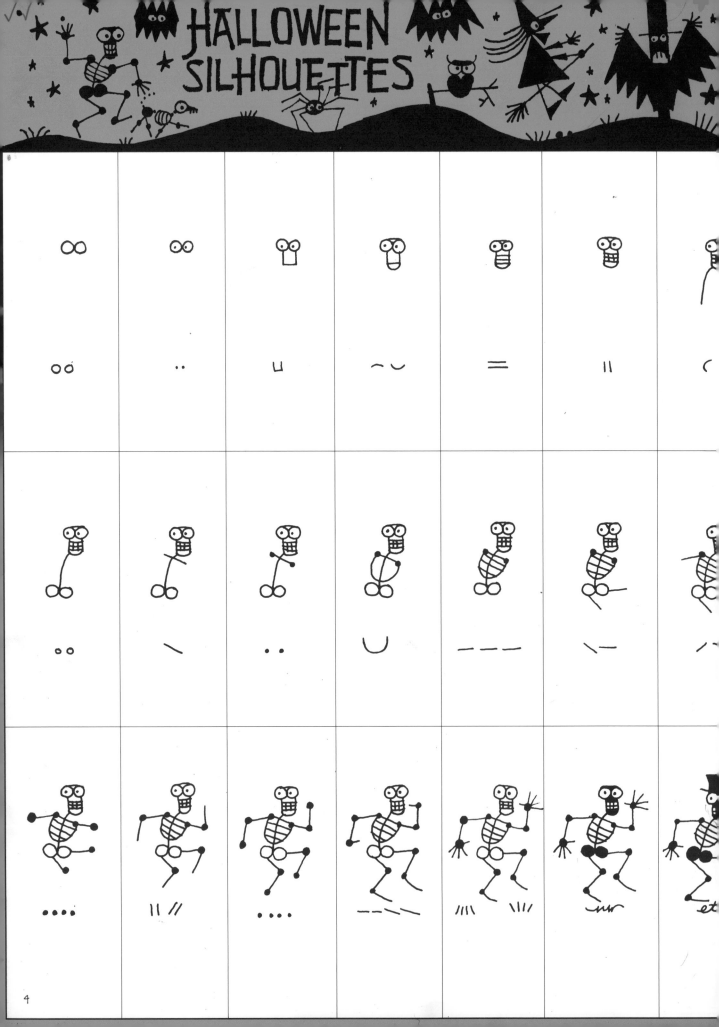

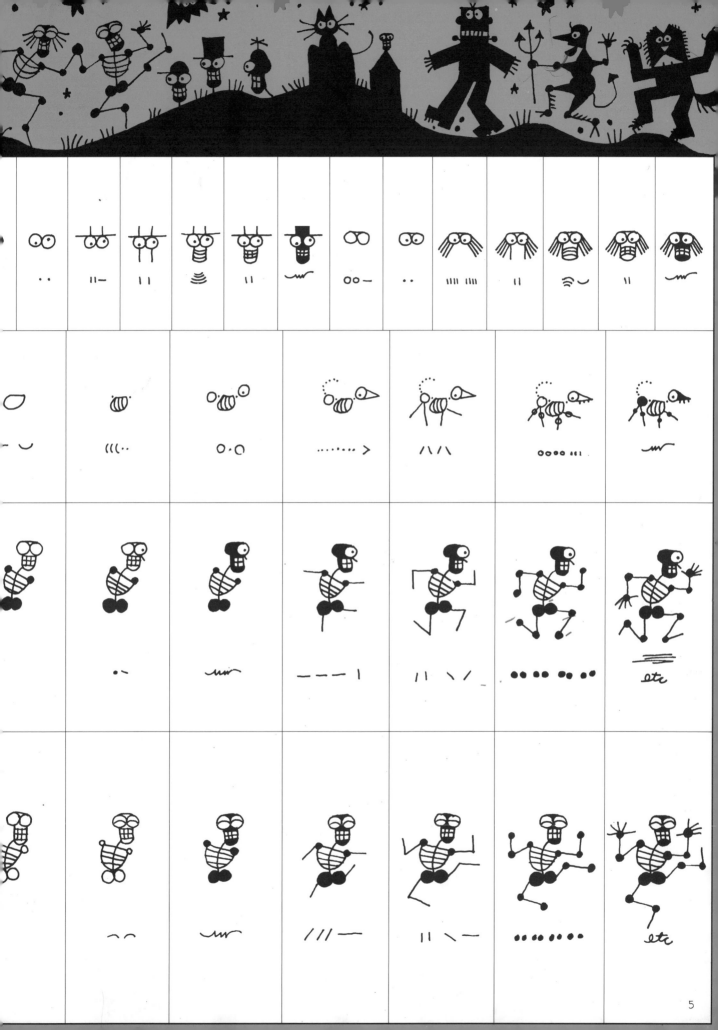

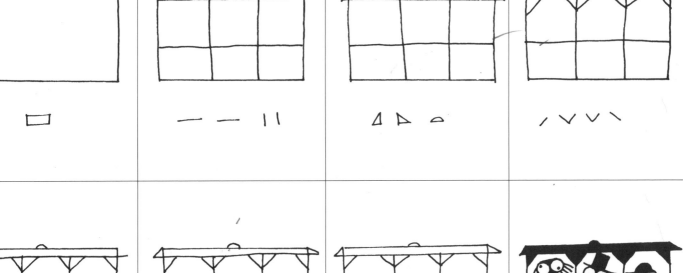

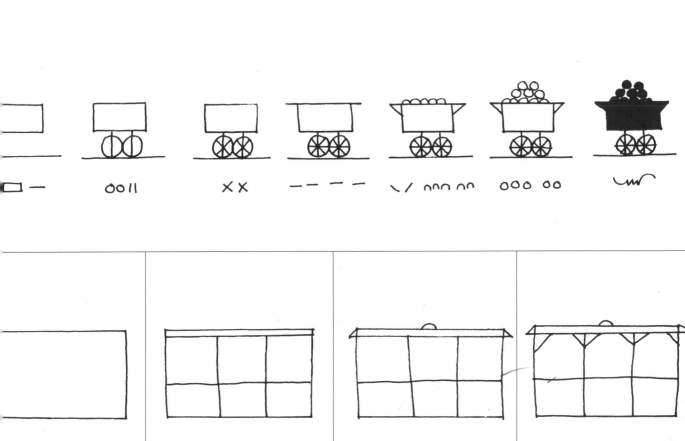

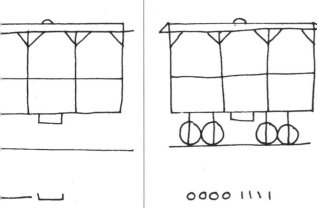

7

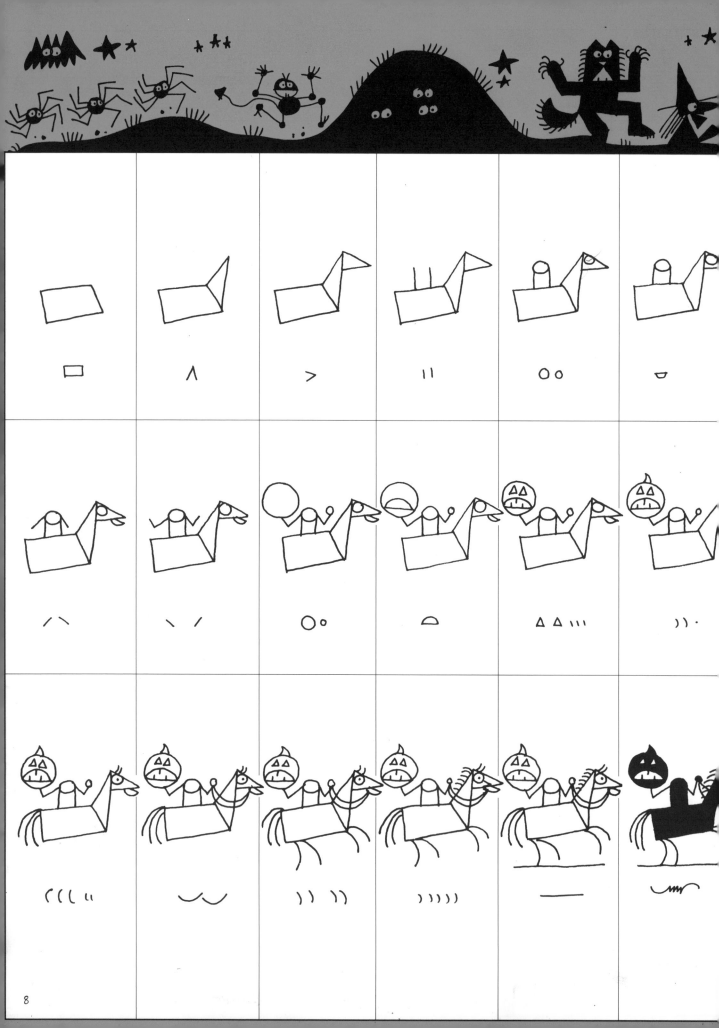

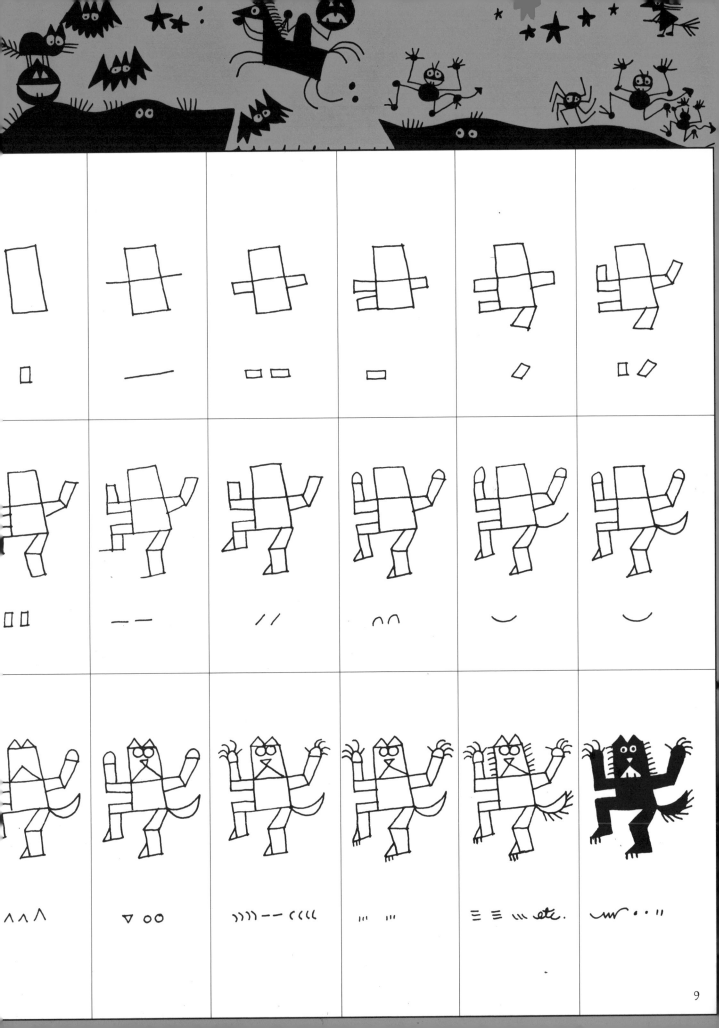

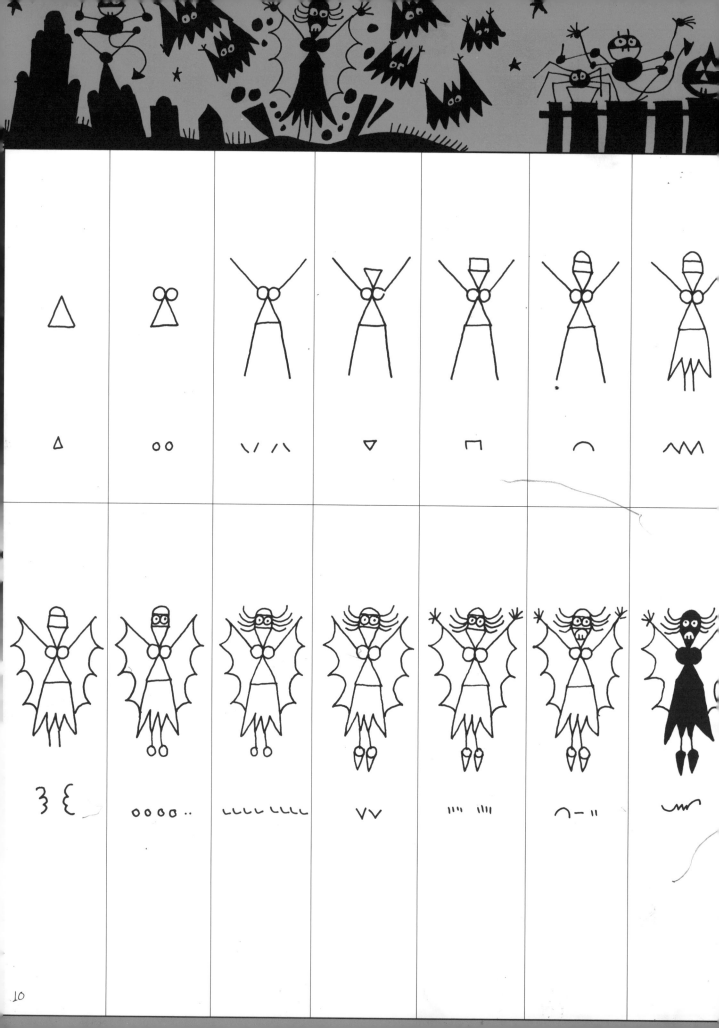

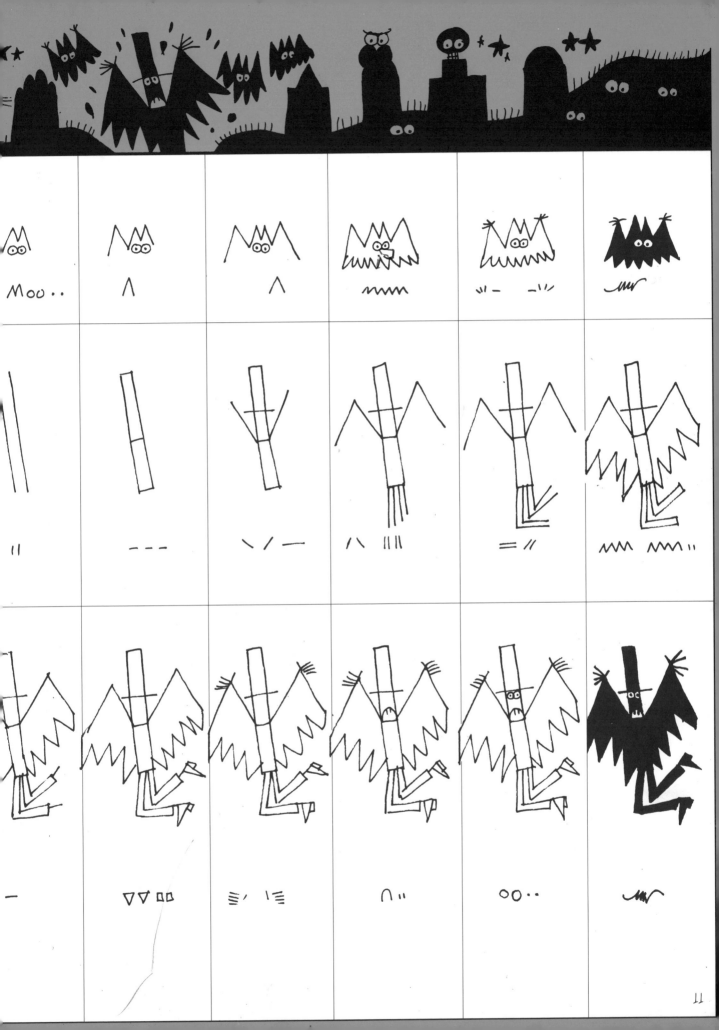

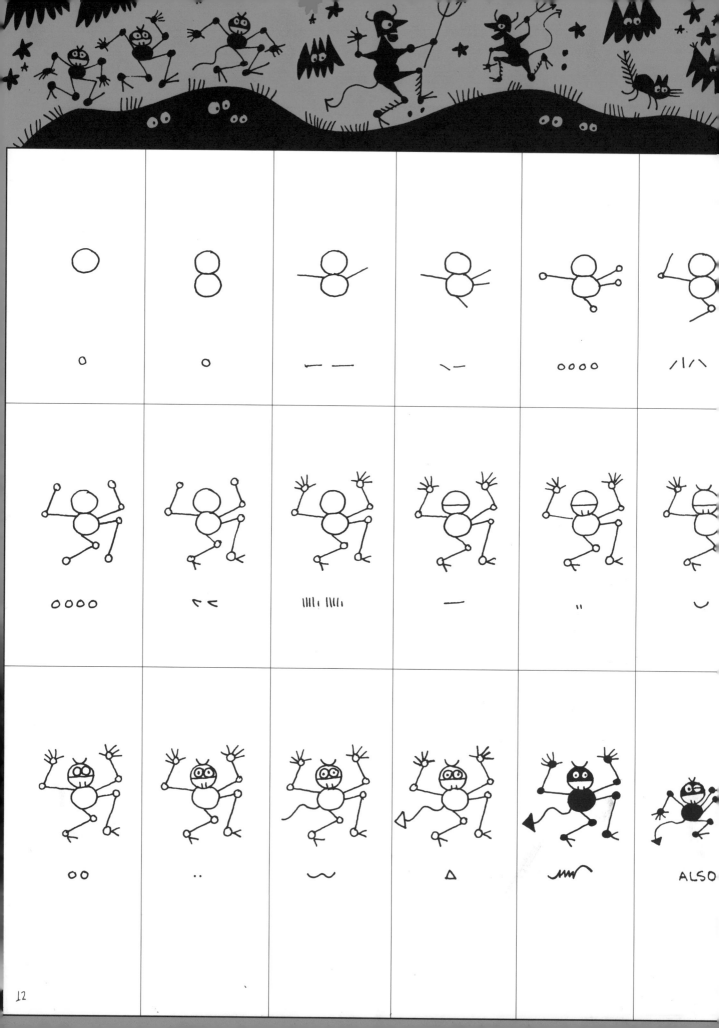

ALSO

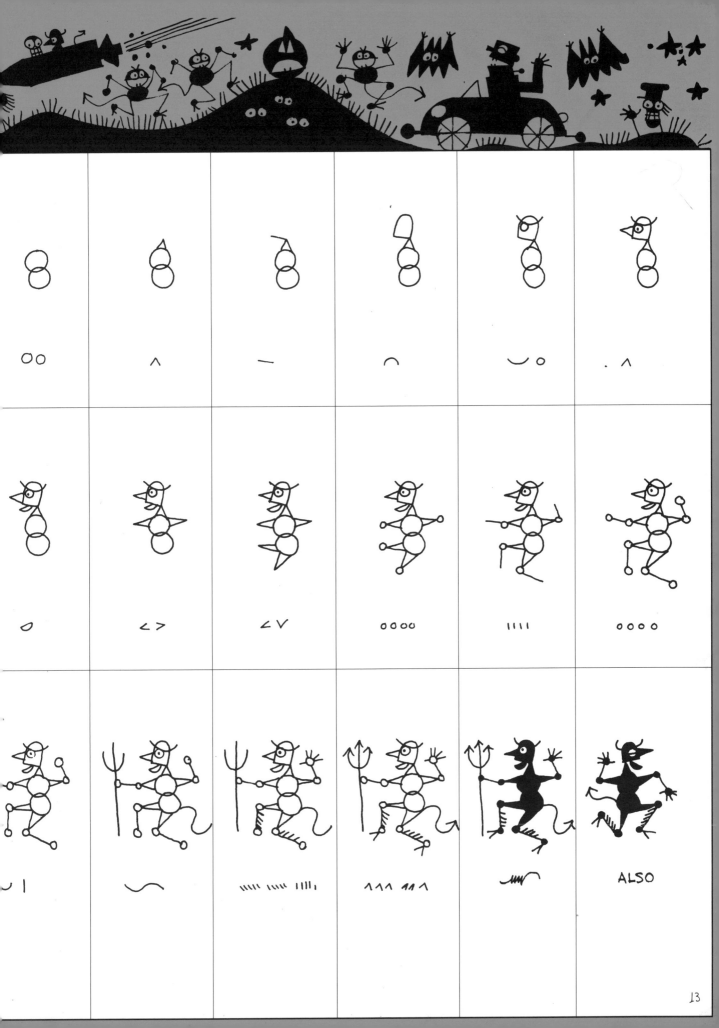

ALSO

13

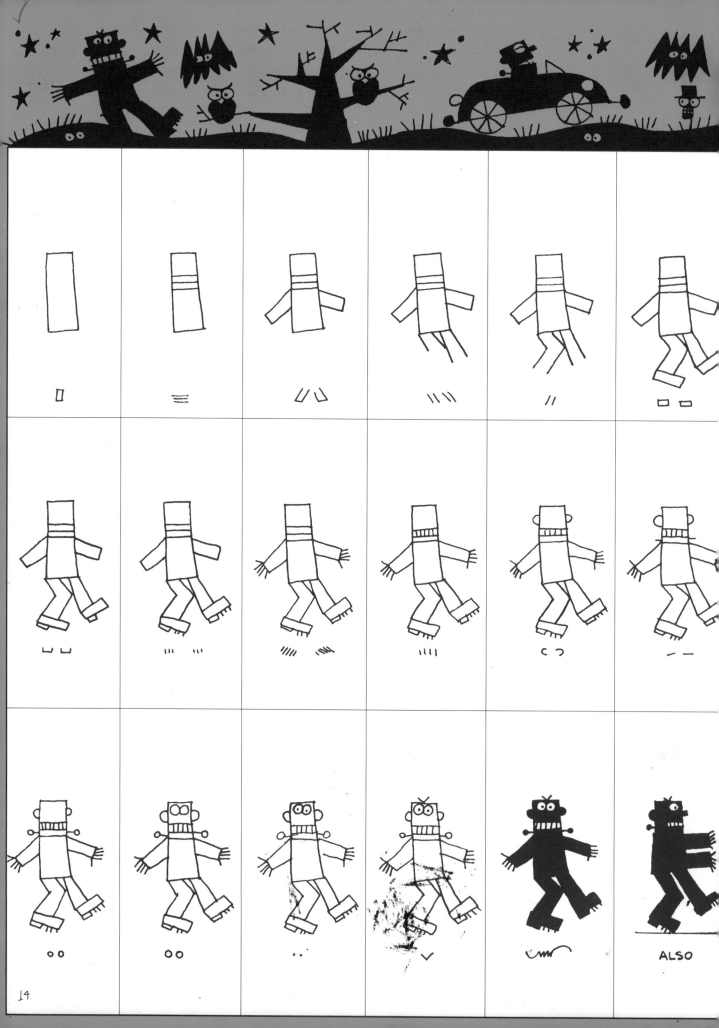

ALSO

14

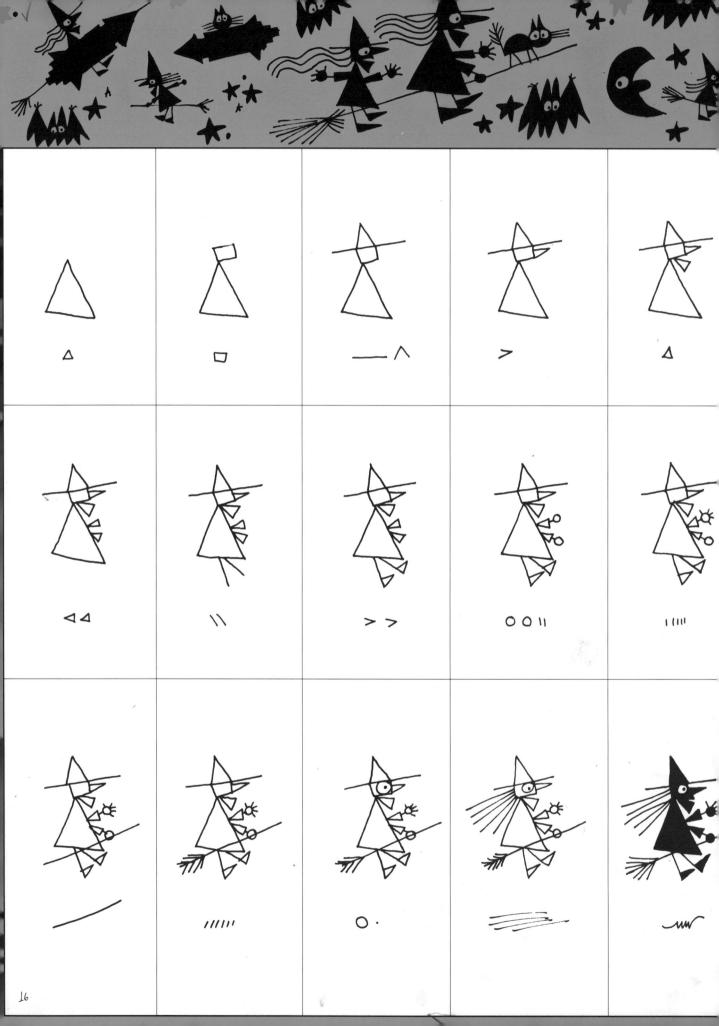

16

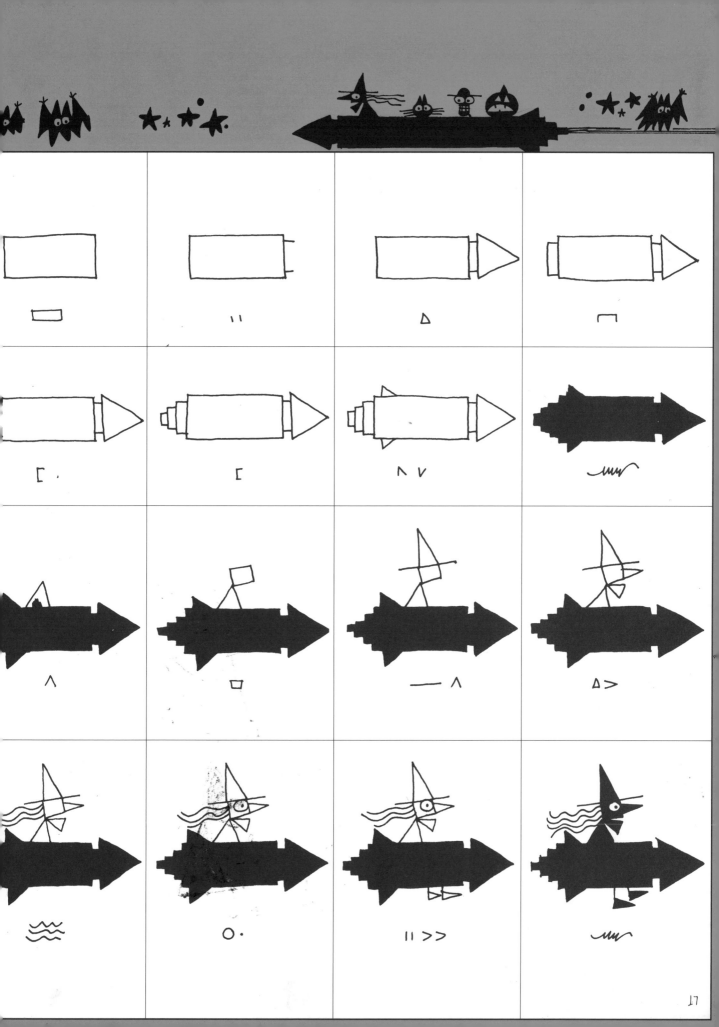

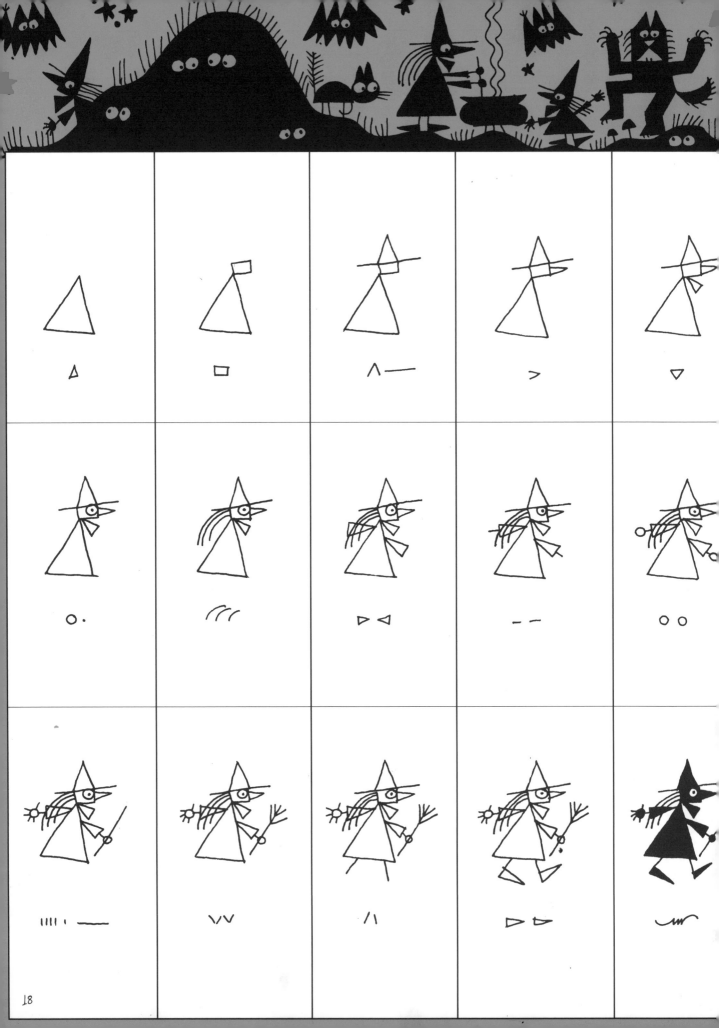

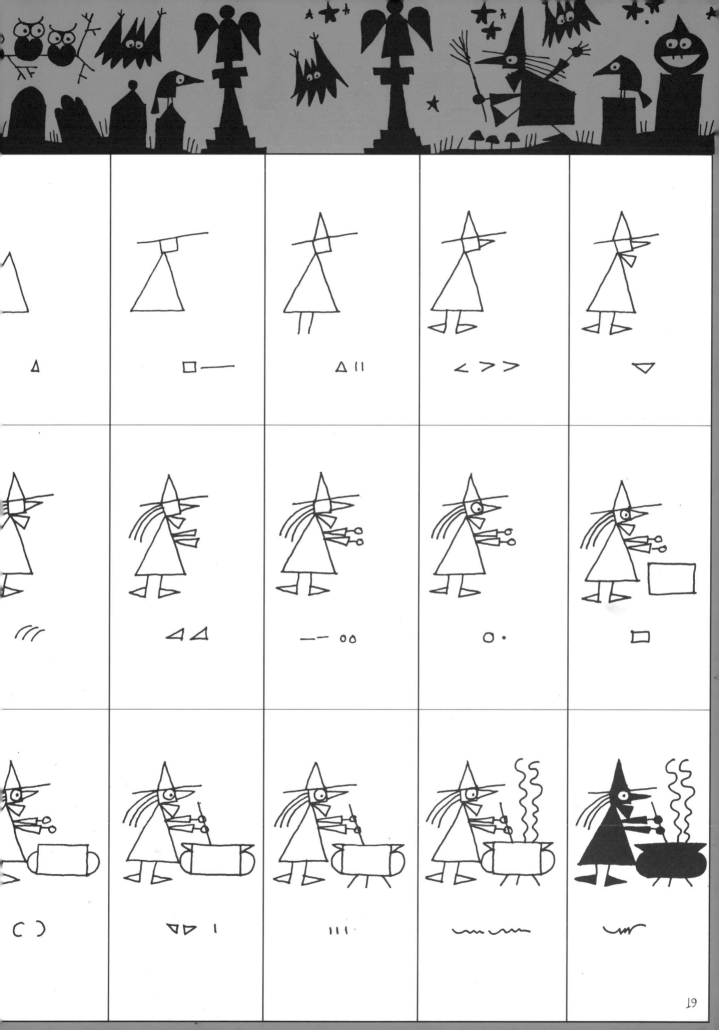

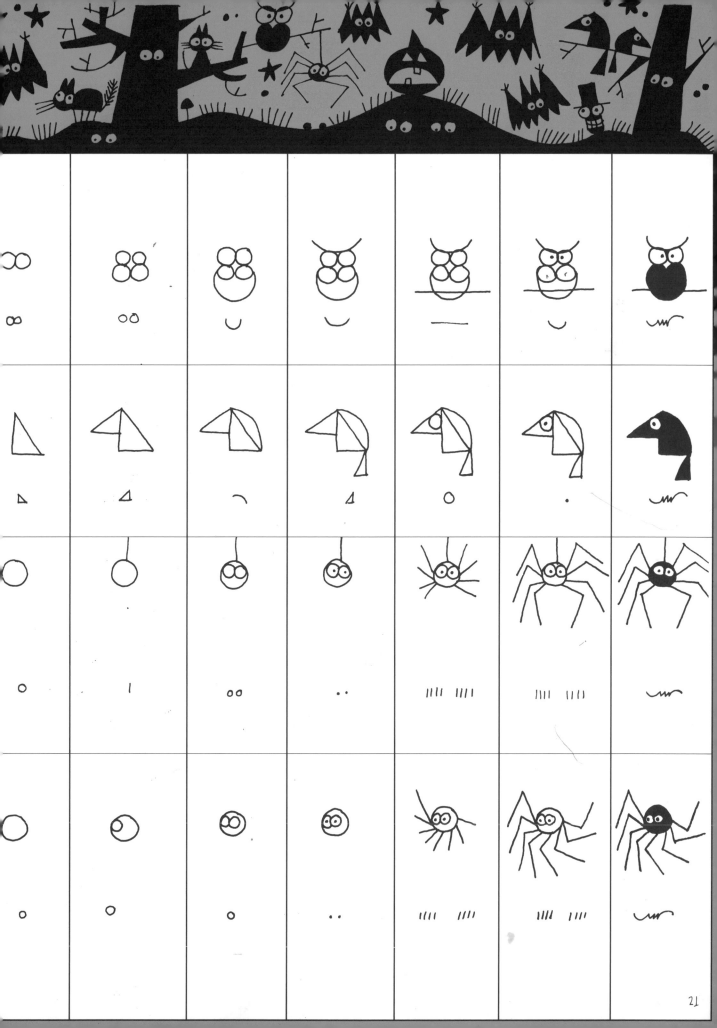

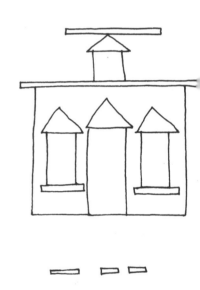

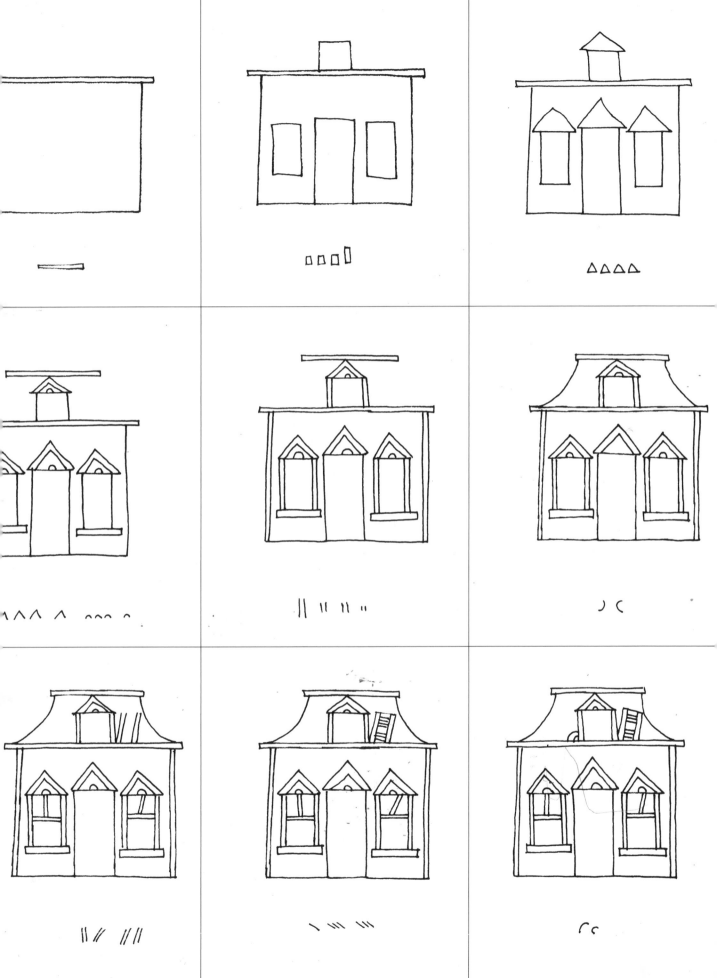

V U etc.

ETC.

24

= ≡ = ⸻ ⸻ etc.

||||||

ALSO

ALSO

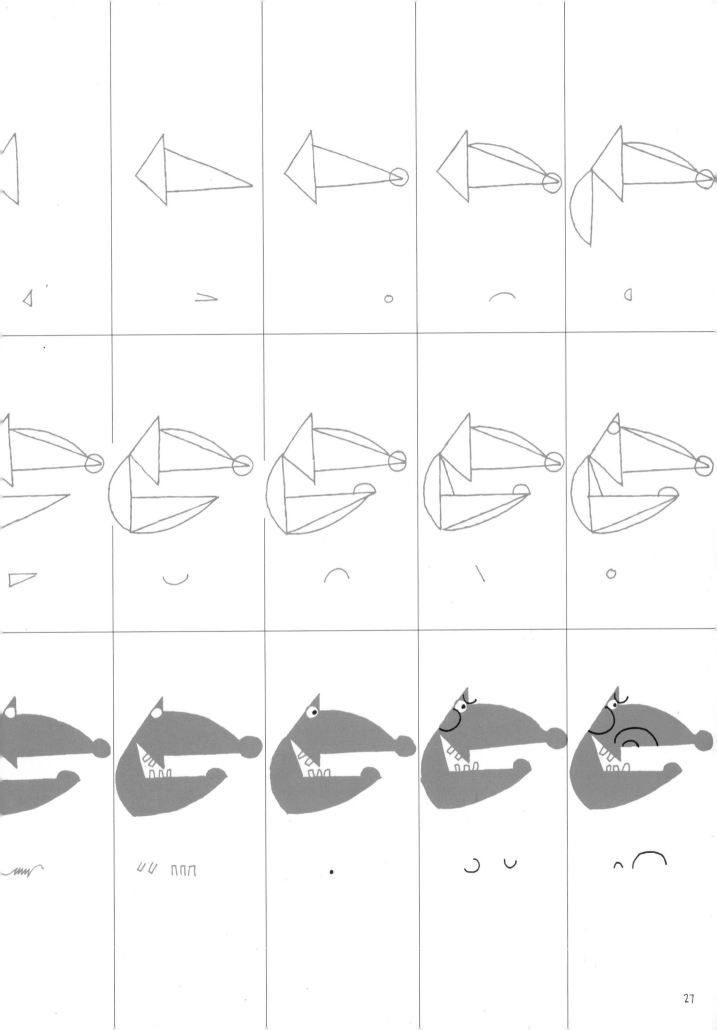

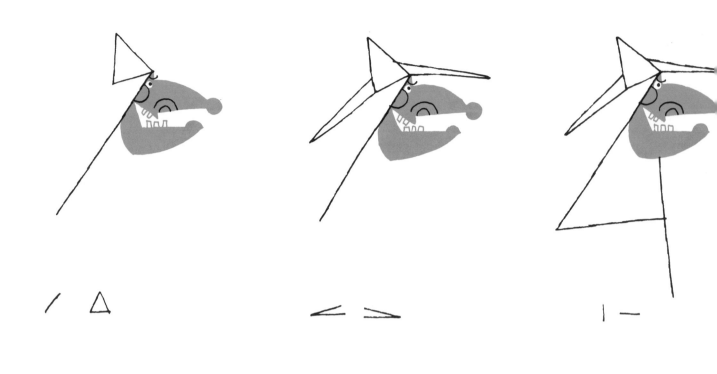

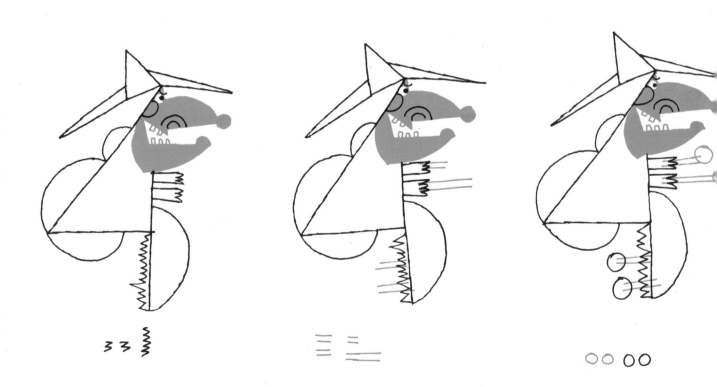

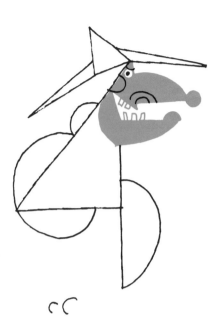
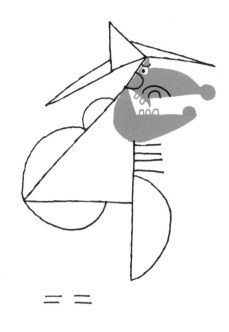

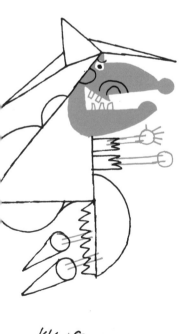
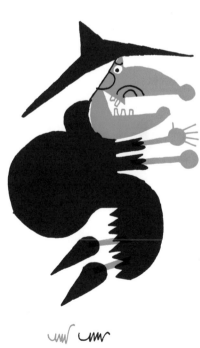

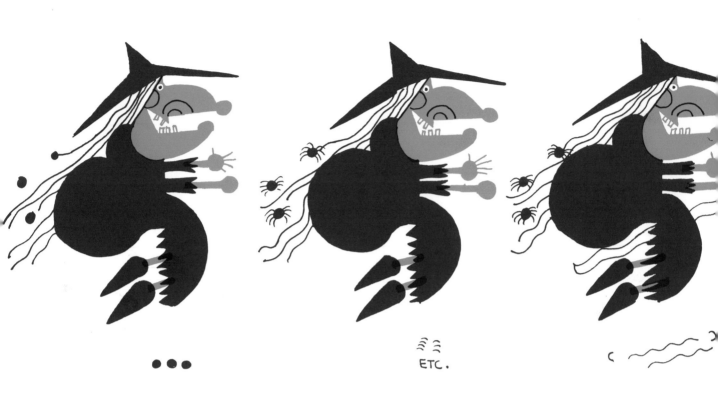

•••
ETC.

30

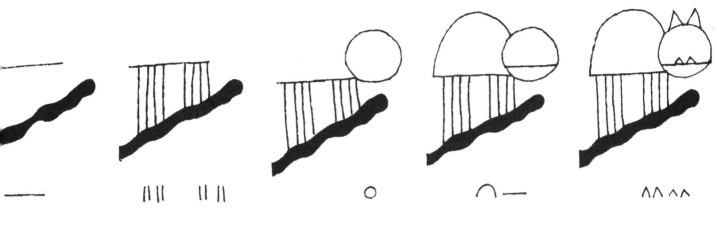

You will find more good Halloween stuff in these other Ed Emberley Drawing Books: